As Seasons Change

J. W. Parr

BookLeaf Publishing

As Seasons Change © 2023 J. W. Parr

All rights reserved.

No part of this publication may be reproduced, stored in a retrieval system, or transmitted, in any form or by any means, electronic, mechanical, photocopying, recording or otherwise, without the prior written permission of the presenters.

J. W. Parr asserts the moral right to be identified as author of this work.

Presentation by *BookLeaf Publishing*

Web: www.bookleafpub.com

E-mail: info@bookleafpub.com

ISBN: 9789357742498

First edition 2023

To You,

Who dreamed but struggled to believe.

ACKNOWLEDGEMENT

Thank you to God, my family, and my friends for inspiring me, encouraging me, and motivating me to continue chasing my dreams, even when I doubt myself. Thank you especially to Jamie and Elsie, who push me to be the best man, husband, and father that I can and who never stop believing in me. I love you all.

PREFACE

As we grow older, so much in our lives change. Our thoughts, our feelings, our actions, our beliefs, our loves, our passions, and countless other pieces of what makes us human. Sometimes these changes make us better people, sometimes they make us worse. Sometimes we don't even realize that they've taken place unless we take an opportunity to sit down and reflect.

I believe that there is great importance in reflection. Not in looking back with regret, because nothing we can do will change the past. But through reflection, we can see where we came from and all of the battles and struggles we've fought through in order to shape ourselves into who we are today, for better or for worse. Then, we can use this knowledge to help guide our current selves in the direction we'd like to progress in. Without taking a moment to consider our past and present, we forfeit any small semblance of control that we might have in shaping our future.

That's where this poetry book begins---roughly 4-5 years ago. As I was selecting and putting together the poems, I was shocked and intrigued to see the natural progression that my writing took. I could see in real time how my writing had been inspired by the events taking place in my life over the last few years, through both the good times and the bad. I rarely take the time to go back and read things that I wrote years ago, but by doing so, it filled me with so many different emotions. But by the end, I came away with a sense of comfort, gratitude, and solace for all the challenges and changes that I'd made it through, as well as for the person that I am today.

Much like life's ups and downs, I decided to split the book into three parts, which I believe will be noticeable, as you travel through themes of loneliness and despair, into motivation and perseverance, and finally into hope and love. And while no one will experience a life full of continuous positivity, joy, and happiness, I hope that my words can help bring some hope that on the other side of pain and sadness, there is fulfillment and contentment to be found.

No matter how dark the night gets, the sun will still rise in the morning.

Dolente

Fashion harder, into stone
This thing that used to beat so beautifully
A melancholy melody has replaced;
A sullen symphony, a cacophony

A song without words,
Without a key or a time
As the ensemble falls into disarray
By the conductor without a baton

I followed you
Even after the tune faded;
Sometimes, I still hear it
Whistling in the wind

And yet, it's a different sound
Lifeless, nonhuman, soulless
An accident of nature
Destined to drift away

Much like you,
The one who stole the noise
From my ears,
From my heart

You & I

Tell me, if it were true

~Save me the time to waste

I'm so lost, what else to do?

~Allow me to find another taste

Just because I leave today

~Doesn't mean that I regret

A single thing I didn't say

~For in the end 'twas best

Just please be honest with me now

~Let's stall the time slipping by

We can both learn to do without

~This thing called You and I

Misguided Hope

3

Tender whispers in the dark
Promising secrets,
Lies, I know, for they will never come.
Sweet words with pure intention,
Hopeful, loving, and yet
Nothing more than misplaced faith.
But not much longer,
Will I keep forging onward
Praying, begging, for a new reality
For sincere honesty,
That I once believed existed.

Though, I don't regret
Being a foolish lover.
Only that my hope,
My faith,
Hadn't been so misguided.

Faux

Vacuous
Empty
But only inside
On the surface
Is a smile
A courtesy laugh
Faux expressive interest
And a welfare check

But small talk
Is forgotten
Along with the face,
The name,
And interest
Taking the fake,
Leaving the real

Peace.

And emptiness.

Liar, Liar

5

How insignificant it can seem —

A small white lie

Told in the shadows,

Lost in the narrows

Until it hits bottom,

Lands among the kindling

To become a roaring fire,

Seeking out the liar

Engulfing every place

In which solace was once found

Till it licks up your very breath

Leaving behind nothing left

Sitting in a Burning House

Although I thought they'd burn themselves out
The fires have only grown stronger
Leaving behind the charred remnants,
The smoking and smoldering ashes
Twisting and scarring the bones
Eating alive the pages of memories
The books we wrote
Nothing but kindling

***

From the smallest spark
It began as a flicker
And still, the opportunity existed
A window of time left to extinguish
But the windows shut, then caught fire
The glass shattered from the building pressure
Leaving behind no chance to escape
All that remains is us
Trapped in place by the enclosing flames
Perhaps, there is one last hope for survival
A way for us to make it out together
And yet,
I might be too scared to even try

At least in the fire,
I won't have to feel so cold

Vertigo

The mountains above,

The stars below,

Whisper into my ears

Ethereal consultants to a lost soul.

Help my misguided steps

Along the innumerous paths ahead,

No matter which I take,

I find myself further exiled.

How then does one spring forward,

To carve a route in stone?

For the mountainside is not engraved easily,

Nor can the star's radiance be contained.

Such difficulties beget disillusionment,

Like a mighty wind that snaps my ship's sails,

Only to abandon me, stranded

In the midst of the abyss.

"Does that mean all is lost?"

I cry out with my last breath,

Pleading for a rope, a simple length of twine

That can steady me.

Awakening

Beckon to that within
Which has lied dormant all these years
That still reflection
Scared, even, to glance from the mirror

The night has drawn too long,
Like a famine across the land
Sunlight must spring forth
You've hearts and minds yet still to enchant

Lo, if time does hinder,
Restraining all that dreamers dream,
Shatter all the clocks!
Let loose consciousness into a stream

Moonlit Sky

Dancing out upon the waves
~Like the swans upon a lake
Glimmering through the deepest gloom
~Such a lovely sight to take

With every ripple, I hold my breath
~Like waiting for a storm to pass
And when the vision becomes clear
~I pray for it to last

To see such beauty is a rarity
~Yet, a gift you give so freely
I long to taste your cooling spirit
~So I find myself still kneeling

No matter how long I wish for time
~And hope this night won't end
The first rays of fresh heat shine out
~A new day now to begin

Surety

Every year that passes by
Brings thee ever closer
That with which
I knew not of
Until time found me older

Yet ever since its grip
Found me, held me tight
No matter with what strength
I try to fight
Never have you left my sight

For the Virtuous

Trying harder, to reach further

Letting go of the fake,

Unripened fruits

Holding out for what lies in wait.

For the golden apple

Hides among the branches

Only appearing to,

Granting access to,

Those that can find it,

Those with virtues:

Patience;

Determination;

Steadfastness

Closing Time

Cast away your doubts
Breathe deep and full,
Like a gentle tide's pull
How did we live without?

Lessen the tears within
Turn back the pendulum
Reminisce those internal hums,
Start anew again

Perseverance

To speak some words
From beaten lips
Is not a job
For cowardice.
Like how the truth's
Kept from the light
Since a shadow spreads
The bigger lie.
Run from the pockets
Of Mr. Greed
Before he sells you
What you don't need.
No matter how good
The bakery smells
They only care
If your soul is for sale.

Just turn your back,
And plug up your ears
You'll be better off
If you never hear.
For the lies they spread
And the souls they steal
Can make anyone question
What's fake and what's real.

Stay the harder path,
It's all for the better
Remember that the strongest
Have the most hell to weather.

Sacrifice

Much should be said
Of the giving of oneself
To listen, slow to speak
To struggle, week to week
Asking for nothing else

A smile on the face
Despite the deepening lines
Is built on love and care
Is meant to grin and bear
Regardless of the times

Where we are now
Doesn't lie with the truth
Isn't meant for little ears
Isn't cause for their tears,
Calls for false proof

Understand why it's done
From the purest intent
To help to ease the minds
To nourish and to make kind
All those Heaven sent

A Walk Through the Woods

Meet me in the woods,
Underneath the tallest trees
Where the leaves are growing, green
And the flowers begin to bloom.
Taste the sweetness in the air,
As it whips across your face
Prompting a smile, a laugh
While even the sunlight gets jealous.
Take my hand and I'll lead,
Before we dance across the floor
Littered with the brightest petals,
Your dress floating around you.
We'll drift into the darkness
Lit only by the full moon,
Making plans for tomorrow
And for when we'll come again.

Harbinger

Come to me
Across the broken waves
Through the hidden mist
I'll be waiting

Let the stars be your guide
Between the empty black veil
Like a cosmic compass
Back to me

I may grow old, waiting
As time passes by so quickly
A flicker of light
A grain of sand

But I will not falter.
I await you nonetheless
Longing to hear your song again,
Like a calm mountain hymn

Oh, comforter, I assure you
I'm ready now,
As I'll always be
For our reunion

Hope Blossoms

Down another road
Or is it the same?
It feels like I've been here before
At least a handful of times,
And yet, something's different

It's less lonely here now
The road, the path, that was so worn
Has been paved over, smooth and easy;
Like the sound of tires rolling down a brick
road,
There's a soothing element

Although, I still can't shake this feeling
This nagging worry
The fear of "getting too comfortable"
The fear of ending up back on the old road,
Lonely, cold, and tired

But no, I must set my eyes forward,
To the sun on the horizon,
On the brand new day;
I'm not walking alone anymore,
A new hope blossoms inside

Birth & Rebirth

Dreaming of you could never touch
The reality of the moment
No word could tell the tale
Of when my heart was stolen

What an unexpected feeling
To be changed in an instant
To search for your former self,
Yet see them in the distance

The giving up of freedoms,
An unwelcome sacrifice
Blooms into contentment,
A most fulfilling life

Love is an Ocean

To feel the river flow
Crashing against the rocks
Currents blend together
Beneath the riptides
Drawing in, pulling out
A beautiful, powerful mixture
Two forces in synchronicity
Tangled up inside a
Never-ending torrent
As if brought together
By all the forces of nature
All at once dark and terrifying
Beneath a stormy sky
While clear blue and peaceful
Reflecting a bright sun
No matter the rainy days
Or the fairest weather
The current never stops

Star-Crossed

High above us, in distant lands
Lie fields of stars
Burning brightly in their own expanse
All alone in the crowded infinite
Building slowly toward something more,
That which will be seen by no one
Yet still they strive for a reason,
Their purpose for existence

Though, perhaps
In this wild universe
The two of us
Could help end their search

For if a star
Needs but to shine
I, myself
Need but your hand in mine

Weightless

I once used to dream

Of what it would be like

To float on top of the clouds,

To soar like a bird,

Or, perhaps, a balloon,

Through the wide open sky.

To never have to look back down

Or feel the way that I used to,

Back when gravity seemed to be

Chaining me to the earth.

But no longer do I have to dream,

Or imagine a weightless flight.

For I feel the wind upon my face,

The rushing of air beneath my wings

Because since the day I met you,

My feet haven't touched the ground.

www.ingramcontent.com/pod-product-compliance
Lightning Source LLC
La Vergne TN
LVHW010842200726

843508LV00012B/2719